"Heart of a Woman-Pain"

Jerry D. Hayes

"Heart of a Woman

" Poetry

"Dedicated to the woman have shared their lives and stories with me. Hopefully you will not be disappointed by the poetry that represents the stories."

A special thanks to Judy A. Thurston for her editing and positive feedback on the poetry and pictures. Pictures from Pompeii, Italy.

A Little Girls Questions

Walking to the refrigerator and wondering what there is to eat
Opening to the doors there is no milk, fruit nor is there meat
On to the pantry and still looking for some food
Growing sadder by the moment is becoming the mood

Putting a chair up to the counter so I can look
I had to find something to help, the telephone book
Climbing on the counter I opened the doors
Hoping to find something to eat for sure

There was no food in the house today
But where was my mother and why didn't she stay?
Always running off to some faraway place for fun
Trying to find the next glow in her life and then some

I am a little girl this should not be so hard to find
Maybe I should go to the neighbors, would mother mind?
I am growing hungry by the moment can she not see
That I cannot concentrate in school, that little girl is me

Why does my mother go out all the time?
Why it only the pastor and the nuns who are so kind
Today, I am a grown up woman with a beautiful face
Surviving my childhood only by others love and grace

A Poetic Mask

Hiding feelings behind a well versed mask
Questions there were that one really wanted to ask
How in real life being so peaceful and so calm
Then writing poetry until the early morning dawn

Feelings that exist that are hidden so what does one believe
Showing them to others or are they worn on my sleeve
Would you like to know that there are times that I really do cry?
Knowing pain and there were times inside one was wanting to die

Would you be happy to know that one can be so sad?
Experiencing anger and being really upset and mad
Helping you, will all of this to understand the person you see?
Helping you to know that person that really exists inside of me

Realizing that in person, looking always with my eyes
Ears opening to everything, much like some type of spy
Aware so keenly of the things that are all around
Listening even to the smallest kinds of sounds

Thoughts so many that runs throughout my mind
Please just be patient and just to me be really kind
The Mask is something that's been worn very well
Trusting however, when telling you, it is nothing but a poetic shell

A Father's Love

Lord, I hated to go
As I could see my last moments moving fast
Moving slow

Lord, I hated to go
Would she understand how much I loved her?
Now I would not be able to show

Lord, I hated to go
Would she find out all about me?
All the things I wanted her to know

Lord, I hated to go
I just want her to have the love
I had for her and I let it flow

Lord, I hated to go
Did I give her a chance to survive?
Or would life make her down and low?

Lord, I hated to go
But would she find the love
I wanted to give her and to sow

The Lords Response

She loves you still deep inside
But her love for me she will never hide

Alone Now

Many years having passed since being truly alone
Many days and nights experiencing and this is known
Feeling not the need to grasp on to someone to really care
Feeling some sadness and knowing some feelings of despair

Learning that happiness is something that can really exist
When others demand that attention that finding one can resist
Going and deciding what one wants in this life and able to decide
No longer having to shelter thoughts or any else to hide

Now when I am all alone in this place I sleep
There have been moments that I can be sad and weep
Not because of the one I lost and did not keep
For it was sown deep in the fears that I did finally reap

Where I go, I always take with me
Happiness that I hope others can always see
I no longer feel that I am totally alone on this earth
For now I am learning to grow with my own self worth

When we talk and when we share
I hope deep inside you know that I really care
Many men know how to touch the flesh of a girl
But all too few to know her heart, her soul and that she is a priceless pearl

Am I Crazy

Am I crazy?
Or just emotional lazy
Desiring to be understood
Doing things that maybe not what one should?

Permeating fears existing in one's life
Caused upheaval and family strife
Ending up the way one is today
When others can be just emotionally play

Being crazy for the way I act?
Would many doctors confirm this fact?
Only wanting to be close to you
All the things wanting us to do

Wanting so many things to express
Maybe alone wanting now to confess
Understanding surely someplace to find
A heart that is extremely tender and kind

Maybe being crazy just today
Telling you everything would you stay?

A Son's Bedtime Prayer

Laying me down now it's time to sleep
Praying the lord for my soul in him to keep
Forgiveness in this prayer now to ask
All things done wrong are all long past

Forgiven and forgotten
Even when occasionally rotten
Making hopefully my mother always glad
Last thing I want is her to be sad

Wanting her always to just be happy
Fun, playful, smiling and just snappy
Please don't for the world her to be afraid
Tell her that her son wants to just come to her aid

Maybe it's just simple; she needs me to help her cook
When her eyes go bad reading her a book
Maybe just keeping my room more clean
Little brothers and sister maybe not to be mean

Grandmother can get me from the school
She and mom seem always really cool
Knowing that you are always for me there
Living in my heart that you are everywhere

Knowing that you will always love me
Growing up to be special that you hope for me

Making my mom safe, happy and sweet
No suffering for her life or her having to weep
Closing my eyes and no longer pretending to be asleep
Trusting my lord with my mom and soul, both to keep

Behind the Mask

You say you're in love with me
Yet there is so much more for you to see
So many words by so many men
Yet you have no idea where I have been

Men think if they use the word "love"
That I will come flying like their little dove
There is a mask I wear to hide my tears
I put it on because of the fears

I do not trust love, I really cannot
So many issues that I struggled and fought
You see the beauty of my face
My lips invite you for just a taste

You say I have a beautiful smile
That you should stay for a long while
I have a nice figure and you like my body
You tell me I am a real "hottie"

Casual words of love I cannot stand
Like noisy cymbals commingled and bland
I do not trust those words today
My heart is not yours to wound or slay

There is only one place a mask is real
One look into my eyes will surely reveal
Do you know of the anger I have had
Did you know the pain of losing a dad?

I will not trust those words of love
When I was pushed, beaten and shoved
I cried so many a lonely nights
Where did mother go so far out of sight?

Then when I let my walls come slowly down
Finally I trusted those flattery sounds
I gave my all too just a few men
But love did not mean the same to them

If you really think you love me and care
Behind the mask you must venture and dare
If you accept what is behind this mask I wear
In creditable joy and love is what I will share

Behind the Smile

Behind the smile one is seeing today
Was once a girl who enjoying singing and play
Once invaders coming into her native land
Parents running and packing and making plans

Putting her into a small baggage on top of the bus
Mother and her leaving in all the confusion and fuss
Soldiers looking for all the people including ones very small
Soldiers looking for people short, old, young and even very tall

Life then becoming a great upheaval
Seeing little good but seeing more of the evil
Thousands of tears knowing in her very short life
Experiencing the pains of growing up with all of this strife

Behind the smile one is seeing today
Roaming soul that seems and seeks a place to stay
Beauty and grace many saying in her they all see
Never understanding pasts and escaping to just be free

Birthdays

She was excited about that Saturday morning.
She had sent out 10 invitations for the birthday party
Not a rich family, in fact sometimes the meals were the same all week
Yet, she decided to that it was time to do something special for her son
It had been a hard two years, she had seen his eyes removed and replaced
She had seen him suffer with a patch for weeks.
She had had to keep him back in school
He had suffered in school and health and she wanted to lift his spirits

A birthday party, spend some money that she did not have
She was excited to give this special gift for him to enjoy
That is what parents do, they make the world special

The morning came and she cleaned for hours
She prepared the games, the cake and a gift
She planned out each moment with thought and care
And then she waited for the time to come
Its minutes before and no one is early
And now its 11 and you know how people can be
Fashionably late and no one would dare

Her excitement started to turn with each minute of the clock
Each second it got closer to that time for the party
She kept wondering whether each person would come
She kept wondering if she had done something wrong

She told her son they would all show up today
And now she was thinking that maybe it's not that way
Maybe one or two will get lost or forget
But surely the rest of them will find the way and stay

Then each minute of the clock that day became a pain
That she felt in her heart and could not explain
She remembers the smile he had on his face
And then she clearly saw some concern begin to grow

How could they all not show up today?
Did they not understand how much this meant to her and her son?
Where were all these people today?

Excitement to pain, she knew for sure
30 minutes later to her dismay there came a knock of the door
It was buddy woods, the son of his teachers that year
Buddy woods came to a party, a party of one

The party did not last long that day
Even Buddy did not want to stay
He called his mother to pick him up
But he had some gifts, for him being stuck

She was crying on the chair, when he returned back in the door
She was sad and had so much despair
She felt her heart had been broken with pain
It's the way that a parent cares and question is the world fair

She felt the love from her son
Who kissed his mom and thanked her for trying
That he loved her much and there was no need crying

She always found a way to stay busy that day
She pretended that she did not care
She knew life could already be unfair
Busy working, busy doing, anything to not think about this day

Then the phone would ring so loud
Her heart would jump and wonder if she had called
She wanted to grasp the phone by the next ring
She wanted to know who it was and hear everything

She heard the voice and realized it was not her
Each time she went back to what she was doing
She kept thinking to herself that day
I really do not care, I do not dare

I will not be hurt this one more time
I will survive and I will be fine

Each minute of the day she stayed busy doing
If only to kept her mind busy she might even go screwing
The phone did not ring that day for her
She did not find the love she needed that day
She did not find the love she always wants to stay

How truly special this birthday can be
Today is special for both you and me
Sometimes others can wonder but not see

Broken Hearts

Putting tired head softly against unexposed breasts
Comforting, gently loving and finding needed rest
Swallowing all the current pains and hidden sorrows
Losing not all the battles that might come with tomorrow

Listening now to stories from you and more
Seems like more types of stressful relationship wars
Oceans filling with endless and timeless broken hearts
Happening to simple and the smart as they barely seem to start

Broken Hearts hurting and open wounds that bleed
Yearning for another soul finding they feel that they need
Healing harder after breaking apart many untold times
Trusting love not anymore after hearing same old spoken lines

Running fingers through light brown graying hair
Sharing weaknesses at this moment one still dares
Still feeling wimpling hearts beating with a touch from the head
Pretending so often loving from one has gone and now dead

Silently walking and feeling what caused the pain
Dancing away pretenses brief moments of present gain
Resting head on my body not able to see my eyes
One tear revealing at this moment someone wants really to cry

Much love believing and wanting to freely give you
Broken hearts existing as one or forever as two

But A Stranger

I am but a stranger in your life
Discussing the conflicts, religions and strife
A voice briefly heard but never seen
Words floating across a passing screen

Ideas helping to define the places you have been
Encouraging you on the things you can win
Fighting the expressions and passions of the mind
Gentle to the touch and extremely kind

Distant strangers changing the way we think
Lifting us higher in the times that we sink
Never seen but always heard
Thoughts on to paper with the written word

Cambodia

A land of beauty that you must see
Majestic mountains and giant trees
Unknown jungles to explore and find
Be careful for the unexploded mine

Traditions that go back thousands of years
Millions of families and billions of tears
Tortured memories of the fears forgot
Shallow philosophies that the Angkar taught

Contrasts of the land that I could see
Simple people who lived by the sea
Green trees that cover all the hills
Millions of lives lost in the killing fields

A land of many Buddhist monks and their temples
Living their lives just plain and just simple
Khmer Rouge soldiers came one day
They told the monks they could not stay

Many were taken not too far away
Tortured and murdered the soldiers did slay
Death all around them during these days
People could not protest, not a word they could say

Beautiful face, dark eyes and blacken hair
Her eyes would not at me even stare
A mute, not speaking she did not dare
Her life never seemed to me to be quiet fair

But out of this Cambodian land of pain
Covered by bones and a bloody stain
Tortured memories inside of her refrained
Love was found in two, nothing but gain

Cave

You love the light of day
The warmth on your face
The sunlight you can embrace
This life you have

You love and cherish
What you accomplish
Never to give up
The cave has its draw

You can feel it pull at your mind
Is it a retreat from the sun
When the sun is to hot
Is it a safety and security you seek?

In the deep recesses of this cave
The world does it expect you to be so holy and right
The expectations of so many
Yours the highest of the high

The cave can seem so alone and dark
If you are there all alone
The fears of a world can creep within
Sometimes in the darkness

I want to see clearly and to understand
In the darkness and in the light
The cave is dark and mysterious
But within the cave imperfections are never seen

Your smell can tell you another is there
You can touch and feel something nice and warm
You live on the mountain
But the cave you will always have

But of this you think
When alone and sad.

Closest; When We Know It the Least

I know she loves you lord
This angel you have created
I know she wants to walk and see you lord
This woman that walks upon the earth

Sometimes so confident and in control
And then so insecure and failing
Wanting all that life has to offer
Successes and the failures accepting

Wanting to trust where trust has never been
Wanting to understand those things never seen
How do you show how close to you she really is?
When she feels so far away, not that she is

Coming to understand the greatness you have given her
The fragileness that walks within
When others hear the voice of an angel
Learning how frail she really can be
Sometimes confused and sometimes alone

The voice that can sing
Is the same one that can scream?
You can hear the song
But your heart she does belong
Sometimes it's not the roll she wants to play
She would rather run than stay

Both not sure of the path or the wrath

Cold

Walking into the bar on just that night
Looking at all the people and all the sights
Crowded shoulders and heads that barely appear
One look at a person before in the masses they disappear

Bodies pushing through the crowd place
Barely rooms to stand, or watch, there is no space
Huddled masses of men and women at play
Looking for love for life or just for a day

Beauty she possesses better than the rest
But getting to know her will be the real test
Sometimes people can come off very cold
Realizing it because many times they have been told

But never be too quick to be sure that person is really that way
When they never had a real dad who happened to stay
Children need the love of their parents and more
The foundations of life and developed early for sure

The coldness at first that you might find
Might be a person who is really very kind
Take the time to find out what lies deep inside
With trust and respect, then finding they will not hide

Deathbed

I was lying here sick
It had been that way for months
I knew my time was rapidly approaching
Recently the disease had taken over my body

I started to reflect on my life
The things I had done and what really matters
The accomplishments and the failures

I did not think about the money I had made or
spent
How I could have made more and that that I
wasted
What I thought about was did I provide within a
given standard?
Did we go for want and need?

I thought about my kids
And did I provide them the love they needed
Did I neglect them in their times of need
Did I give them to the tools to survive in today
world
Would they look back years later and thank me
or blame me

I never cared to be rich or famous
But only to look back and know it was a good
life
Where the victories outweighed the defeats
And they could be humble in victory
And strengthened by the failures.

I will look back and think about
The special times I shared my life with you
The things we did
The places we traveled to
The fun times..
The passionate times
The long talks about problems

Moments of frustrations
And years of joy
I will be thankful for the time together
And regret the things that we did not find time to
do or finish

I will wonder if you will find someone to share
your life with in the future.
I will wish for your happiness and joy
I will want you to remember me
I will wonder if you will share all the silly things
we did with the kids and grandkids

I will not think about the mean people of the
world
But rather the fun and interesting ones that we
came in contact with
I will not think about the prideful ones but rather
the humble ones

I will wonder if those words and lessons on life
influenced one child
Whether the things we wrote made a difference
in life
I will ask did I leave this world a better place or
worse?
I will wish I had told some people I was sorry for
the things I had done long before I knew I would
be leaving this world.
I will think of many things. But mostly, I will think
of you.

On my deathbed...I know I will think about you.

The Deepest Soul

Deep within the earth a diamond is formed to be
Intense circumstances and pressure the beauty they will see
Buried beneath of tons of soil and rocks is a heart
Born into pain and hurt from the start

Depression

Men are so attracted to my face and body
They even call me such a "hottie"
The closer they get and came near
The greater becomes of my inner fear

I fight a battle most people can never see
A struggle with depression deep inside of me
So many men think I should belong to them
Because I am attractive and my body so slim

But when you have to spend so much time with me
Love does not come so easy and free
You have to get to know that I am within
Before our love can ever begin

What I ask of you is the time to spend
Developing a love that will never end
Depression scares me to let you know
Afraid that you will run away and love will not grow

Dilemmas

Everyone says that he is a very good man
Maybe it's me that is the one that is hard to understand
Two men in my life now there happens to be
Only one does everyone around me really see

Creating a dilemma that I did to myself for sure
When in the area of the heart I opened that door
One young man is talented and smart
Wanting a new family and a life to start

Wanting to practice in the field of law
Probably he will be wealthy and we will be married by fall
Played in a band and he was very good
Everyone tells me to marry him for me he is too good

Everything in my life I want to be safe and secure
However there is another side that has an allure
Feeling like I must make the right decisions for my kids
Maybe there is only one person that I have to get rid

Finally I decided to let my mind rule my heart
Starting a new direction I would do my part
Life seemed so simple and I wanted to know what to do
But the last decision I did not want to make is living without you

Drifting

Cast on a small raft adrift in the sea
Far enough from the coast line that no one can see
Sinking ship that offered such fun and games
Proving all an illusion and becoming so lame

Riding the waves up and down again
Imaging that this is my ship I continue to pretend
Searching the horizon for another ship or a sign
Water splashing me in the face every other time

Dark, wet, cold and now sitting all alone
Would I have taken the same ship if this I was shown?
Moving in no direction do I feel the raft now has gone?
Wondering how things happen and sometimes seem to go wrong

Drifting in an ocean of water and midnight skies
I can only look from my back to the heavens on high
Realizing that there are billions of stars shining this night
A sense of peace as I drift in this small heavenly delight

Family Pictures

Walking into the room, I saw my father standing there. He was looking at the family pictures on the wall. My father was staring intently at the pictures, examining each one of them. Slowly he would move his eyes from one picture to another. I phased just before I ask him.

"Dad, is everything okay?"

Slowly he turned around and looked at me and reassured me that he was okay.

"Yes, dear, I am doing okay." But he seemed intent on returning to the pictures and examining them. Maybe like he was looking at them for the first, or maybe looking at them as if it was the last time.

"You sure you are okay?" I wanted to know feeling like maybe something was bothering him. But I had always had my father around. You start as a little child and the foundation of your life are those parents. They are the strength and foundation of your life, Parents.

Speaking briefly, as if getting the feeling my father just wanted to be left alone, I decided to go to bed...

Lying in bed I heard my father in the other room as if gasping for air. I was sure it was just a shortness of brief that happens occasionally, or so I told myself. Having an uneasy feeling yet telling myself that it was nothing. Simply nothing.

I waited and waited. Then the feeling would not leave me, so I decided to go and check on my father. There he was on the couch in the living room. Collapsed he was lying now lying lifeless on the couch with a strange look on his face. Fear, Sadness all the emotions flooded my mind as I saw my father lying there on the couch. Dying.

Frantically, 911 were called and they came to his rescue, or so I thought.

A heart attack, but thank god he was going to be okay. Only to find out later when I got to the hospital that he had a second and more massive heart attack that killed him. I had the feeling something was terribly wrong as I walked into the hospital and started to see the family gathering.

The moment you realize that you have lost something important to you, there is such an intense pain that fells your entire body. The permanence of death and separation from someone you love and cherish. The many years of always being there and we come to expect our parents to always be there. Yet, even that is not possible.

For many months I blamed myself for that night. "What if I had gotten up when I first heard the different breathing coming from the living room? I had dismissed the sounds and went back to sleep. Now, looking back, and I am realizing that he was having that first heart attack and maybe if I had gotten up he would still be alive."

"What if?" "What if?"   The guilt built up in me as I blamed myself for not being there at the right moment that he needed me.

Tears and pain are the gifts expressed by the living and a celebration of the love that was exhibited by the love of the person who has passed from this world. The greater the love and influence a person showed us in this life the greater should be the pain and sorrow of their separation from us. For only in the greatest of loves is there found the greatest of sorrow.

Fear of Love

Many people refuse to love because of fears
Rejecting the love because of the history of tears
We start of lives with the great hope of love and joy
But many times find out that we are treated by others like a toy

If love is such a great thing to people so many
Why is it that not everyone wants more and plenty?
How can people really be so afraid of love today?
When they tell everyone around them they want love and say

Those who know not of the love that can really exist
Become so afraid of the pain it might cause and do resist
Companionship, sex and just promulgating our biological seed
Little do they realize that we love out of an innate human need?

Sometimes a woman cannot define the relationship correct
When a man can not possess the woman his efforts she did reject
When we never allow the soul to care and then some
Cold as a winter's stone the heart can become

Firmar Aqui (Sign here)

"El señor podría tú firmar por favor aquí"
Please sign here on this final divorce decree
Many years of trying had just ended in admission of defeat
No longer in my life would I have to withdrawal or retreat

With those words her world separated from me
No longer walking in the door at night would it be her I see
The final act of admitting that we could never agree
Now there is no question that we can go and both are free

But are we free from the memories of the past
Or do they continue in the back of our minds until the very last
Thinking back and wondering if something differently could have been done
Should we have planned more time together just to have fun?

Having much more time now to ponder and write
No longer are my sons around at night in my daily sight

"Apenas un más lugar te necesito firmar"

"Gracias sir, el divorcio será archivado como final"

"Four Cries and Good Bye"

Four times you have made me cry
And for that reason I now say good bye
You do not let me hide behind my walls
And surely caring about you will make me fall

I can see why many might just care
I can see why others might venture to dare
But loving you might cause some fear
Because someone might really want you near

You would surely take my heart and break
Whether you meant to or not I could not shake
It's easy to care about you I can plainly see
But in the end I would want you to love only me

For mine is world that I need to be secure
Not chasing after any kind of mystical allure
Love to me is found in the day to day
Those who make love and those who stay

My children are my life and this I know
That I would do anything to see them grow
They bring me joy in the day and night
They bring me love and a smile at mornings first light

Friends

What does it mean to be a good friend?
Where do lovers begin and friendship ends?
Lovers are not expected to be able to talk
Spending so much time together, finding harder to walk

"Let's just be friends" she wanted to say
Far to much easier to just again push one away
Defining the space that must have a label
Romantic love comes with many naïve fables

Can men and women really be just friends?
Before some attraction that destroys them begins
Women insists that he be "close" before sex he will get
Men afterwards, where is the romance he does soon forget

How many friends do one need to today?
How many will play and how many will stay?
A lover without friendship cannot really last
Coming to quickly and leaving just as fast

Frozen

Seeing only what your eyes want to see
wanting life like only you think it should be
when your hearts not open it is just frozen
Relationships with no depth just a token

You're so consumed with how much you get
you waste your time with hate and regret
thinking that our lives we would share was chosen
When your heart's not open you're broken

Desiring that I can melt your heart
So that we love life our lives never are apart
Thinking that you could give yourself to me
It's your heart that really holds the key

There's no need in placing any blame
You should know I suffer the same
Broken will be my heart if I lose you
Questioning about what I will now do

Love is a bird, she needs to fly
Let all the hurt inside of you die
you're frozen when your heart's not open
why can your open up and let words be spoken

If I could melt your heart
Warmth and love, you would find does start
Frozen is when a heart can't even find the tears
Always buried be your wall of fears

Getting Married

Thinking about what happened so many years ago
Wondering if it was an indication of what it would show
Looking back at how funny it would begin
Predicting also that someday it would come to an end

Good Pain and Bad Pain

Believing that if there are no tears in a person eyes
There is no heart left to love and a person emotionally dies
Where you find tears and someone who cries
You find someone who still cares about others and still ask why

Understanding pain both within themselves and in others
There is no greater pain in life than loving another
Yet even in the pain of love, there is no greater joy
There is no greater connection than between a girl and a boy

There are two different types of pain
It is at this point I probably should explain
Bad pain is the pain felt when hope ceases between two people and does
worsen
Good pain is the yearning to be together when separated from another
person

Bad pain is when souls grow cold, when even the memories are forgotten
Good pain is two souls moving the life boulders together, with efforts soften
Bad pain is when the same arguments happen over and over without any
resolution
Good pain, when a mistake is made and never repeated and each looks
for a solution

Bad pain comes with never being able to forget and forgive
Good pain comes with forgiveness and both have no desire to relive
Bad pain is never missing the person and you don't even make an effort to
endeavor
Good pain is when time never fades the memories of someone you will
cherish forever

Hurting, too

It's late and I am in the darkness
I feel surround by the pain
My soul is tormented and in despair
I should have been happy today
I should have rejoiced in the pleasant words
I should have been having so much fun
The games, the food and the drink

My circumstances if I had used that gauge
Should have been having such a great time today
And yet, I was not happy
In fact, I am very sad today

How can I be glad?
When someone I care about is in so much pain
She is not happy and her soul is leaking
I said that I would never try to repair that soul
That I would never try to fix one thing
That has been damaged
That is so deep within her

Oh god. That tonight I could take her pain
That I could share the burden that she feels within
The sadness she has felt
The pain she knows

She does not even know that I am alive right now
Her focus is on her pain and sorrow
She only wants to fight this battle by herself
Feeling that no one else can know her pain
Feeling like she has caused the pain of some many who love her

We ask her, we plead with her. Share this sorrow, gave us your pain.
But her eyes are focused on the plan she has
Her brain is wrapped in the battle that must be fought
"Do not distract me "and "do not mislead me"
I have listened to you all before
This battle, I will fight and I must win.

"I am alone. And no one can see
What has happened to my soul?
Leaking out, filling the lives with sorrow around me"
She says

She does not know and cannot feel those around
How they hurt
When she hurts
Yet she can feel the pain of those who hurting
Like those can feel the pain she feels

It says that while you were in the garden that night
You prayed drops of blood
Now I can see, that is was the pain you felt of so many
Of those around

How you must have felt the pain
Of others
Of me
Of her

Hurting

I had a great day today
There was fun and joy and play
I saw an old friend and made some more
We drank and talk and played some pool

I can be the life of a party
Getting everyone to laugh and talk
Yet beneath the smile there was a pain
Hurting that I could feel deep inside myself

Walking away and be alone
Thinking about this pain
I was not me and this was plain

I felt so sad and almost mad
Why did I feel this way?
Why did I care so very much?

I spoke that I saw despair
I promised I would never fix
I said I would never see her a broken and in need of repair

I Still Love

I come bowing very low as I kneel
I come asking for many things to heal
Never far away from my god so high above
A father in heaven that I find that I still love

I many times that I would run away
Because it was such a hard battle to stay
No man wanted that love to really work out
Tears inside, hope created and that ended in doubt

If there was ever a time I wanted to succeed
It was with that person who had such a huge need
Just to one a single individual who never understood?
Who if she had realized that we really could

Sometimes families look so perfect from afar
And if they get much closer they will see an emotional scar
One says this and the other says that
They can ever learn how to fight over a cat

Was it really a battle between two people?
Which church to go to and even in choosing a steeple?
Even our views on our god we could not decide
And try as I might in my room to hide

I did not rob nor did I steal or kill
But I come asking for many things of God's will
Never far away from my god here below
A father in heaven that his love he will show

Illusion

Like the great illusion she play again and again
This is the only way that she can pretend
Love's great call that she feels that she once had
When the only truth is that it was all very sad

Tell a well man that he is fine and he knows it
Tell a sick person they a ill and you can never show it
People believe that they want to exist in their own minds
Maybe it's the only good thing they have that you will find

Taking a great journey one day I did suddenly begin
Only to find that it was only a lie that never ends
The mind is a place where dreams and reality both go
Time is the master of which one is real for others to know

Silence

Strange mixtures of thoughts filling my mind
Unsure where to start this late sleepless night time
Silence
Brewing strands of confusion developing many strands of thought filled
lines
Feelings of joy, anxiety, love, excitement and even fear I might find
Untapped emotions waiting for release and waiting on a sign

All these feelings wrapped up inside the depth of me.
Which direction is the best I hope to see?
Silence
I don't know to go either left or to the right
Adventure, new friends and new places is one choice that might delight
Bringing new taste and sensations that produce a high I might

Do I go back to the old familiar feelings that I knew
One that I have loved and left once before I flew
Silence
Confusion is embracing me, not sure what I should do
Reaching out to others in answers I am looking for clues
Wanting the right answer for the love of one or is it two?

Time passes and is too precious to waste
Wondering if my decisions will bring happiness or a bitter taste
Silence
Contemplating many aspects of my life, my thoughts I fight
Speculating if I should go left or right.
Sitting here in the darkness of the moonless night

In Stillness of the Mind

Beating of my heart and my mind is still
easily forgetting events normally would I feel
Love's exciting purity when it first begins
Sadness when love's purity does always seem to end

In Stillness of the Mind

Does unselfish love really exist?
Can a man not be selfish and really resist?
Idealism persisting through the tempest of life.
Believing someday that I will be a wonderful wife

In Stillness of the Mind

Finding quiet assurances, inner peace, at my core
Facing doubt, loneliness, and anxiety,
Harsh realities without honor or piety
Because of these challenges to my essential being.

In Stillness of the Mind

Sensing the basic side of all humanity,
Knowing others to allow me peace and sanity
Fearing and distrusting, separating from the love of friends.
Trusting others, accepting and enjoying others to the end

In Stillness of the Mind

Richer my life will be for comfort than now from you
Accepting, helping others to be more and to be true
Willing to be more able and accepting of me
Knowing how much life is giving to me

In Stillness of the Mind

History of my heritage, and a loving families touch
needing greater trust and realizing how much
Opportunities in life that I have been given
Urges in happiness of live to other not should be hidden

In Stillness of the Mind – thinking these thoughts

Just a Memory

Living our lives as we go about today
There will be a time that we cannot stay
Twinkling like a star high in the sky
Happening to us all that someday we will die

Living our lives like endless bank of days
Worrying and stressing and only occasionally to play
Touching lives we encounter as traveling along life's way
Realizing things are not black or white but shades of grey

Leaving is inherent in the love we find
Months, Hours and years or just even a life time
Impressions and pictures created on another's mind
Hateful and evil or others that is good and kind

Gone and forgotten may you never be
Maybe just a memory of someone much like me

Labels

Rich bitch, spoiled, wicked, slut, talented
Fagot, nigger, wetback,
"Born again", evil, brat, witch,
Smart, rich, poor, average
Flirt, horny, sexy, babe
Juvenile, drug, scrub,
Plebe, prep, conservative, democrat or republican
Adulteress, married, single, separated, and divorced
Loving, misogynist, Jew, Muslim, Hindu, Arab,
Woman, man, BI, gay, lesbian
Brilliant, politician, back-stabber,
Hypocrite, religious, righteous, fun
Playful, broken, depressed, sad
Mean, hateful, encouraging
Drunk, alcoholic, bitch
Homeboy, nerd, geek, strange
Sick, broken, paranoid

Use me and you do not have to understand me
It is easier to wear me
Than to know me inside

Lazarus Lives

Days seem so endlessly coming and going
Whatever I try does not seem to be flowing
A restless soul, fog filled density that surrounds me
My eyes reaching out to piece this veil and to see

The world is changing rapidly swirling around me
A mental bondage that pleads to be free
Wondering how others manage to succeed
When deep inside I know I have this need

Raising my leg and then my hand
There is no motion in my actions I cannot plan
Wondering if there is anyone who really will hear
Wondering if there is anyone who understands my fears

Looking Back at my mere Existence
From a humble background of subsistence
Visions of those around me did pity take
Thinking that I would come to nothing make

Just shaking their heads, in silent wonder
will she make it to the very next summer
Sometimes I think that life is not fair
or do others deep inside really care?

Tears rain as a summer storm inside of me
But I hide them well so others will never see
my broken spirit and soul wearily wonders
is there a place in heaven that I can slumber?

Locked in this prison of the life that was given to me
wondering if there was anyone who could bring me the key?
I have not given up on the person I think I can be
But Lazarus did raise and again this you will see

Let Me Go

I know that you are very afraid
Decisions that we have both now have made
I realize too that you are very scared
Thinking that I had not really cared

Sometimes thinking that life is not fair
Splitting up and do we dare?
We both realize that this will not work and both can see
Please just allow me at this time to be free

Maybe someday from a distant shore
I will realize how the relationship could have been more
I wanted you to love me and this is very true
I ever know there was much more I could do

For each of us, I hope we develop a peace of mind
And just maybe experience that love we both wanted to find
Deep in my heart, I can say that I really do love you
But parting in sorrow, somehow I also always knew

Life

At first, I was scared and frightened

The idea of life inside me
The world is a dangerous place I see
What am I going to do?
And the only person I can blame, is you

Privileges and pleasures surely will hide
But now I have a life inside
Future unknown and uncertain life
My youth was spent in so much strife

Then, with months I started to change

The idea of life inside of me
The world with you is a safer place I see
What are we going to do?
Only person I can share this with is you

Freedom not as important as they used to be
We now become a larger family of three
Large my stomach is that all can see
Can this really be the new me?

Your head on my stomach we felt her move
No more dancing for me, no more groves
Nine Months is by far way to long
To hold my child, for her to belong

Finally, I am not afraid or sad
Because I know you will make a great dad

Looking Back

Looking back on all you've been through
Always trying to do the best for us you would do

Years of your youth flying by so fast
Remembering the bad and wondering how did you last?

Your life has not been easy struggling through so much
Always being there for us and giving us that mother's touch

Thanking you for being there through all our stuff
Knowing we gave you a grey hairs and been at time rough

Hoping you know you're made us feel loved
you're a mother that was truly sent from heaven above

maybe not a poet that is really very good
Desiring that you know, your daughters cherish you as much as they could

Something about Mary

Each day I would raise and wash my body
I loved the water and to feel so clean
Now my body smells so inviting
The finest dress, over my breasts, enticing

I look in the mirror without a smile
Work is only but a walk to a mile
Later, I will laugh and tease
But there is no joy as I have to please

Eating my morning meal I stay
I wonder whom I will see today
Some in a hurry and some say just bend
Others I close my eyes and just really pretend

Walking that mile to work in a place
Until my lovers caresses my body and face
Waiting for lovers here I will the time
That they find so fine

One day a lover told me of him
Dismissed it as nothing more than a whim
But I know men they are all the same
I had to go see what his game was

I found him to be strong and tall
Neither handsome or ugly, pudgy or small
But there was something in his face
That had told me the wonder of his grace

Closer I found that I needed to be
Would he want and also desire of me?
And what would I see
What kind of man would I find him to be?

No trust I did have because inside I was mad
I did not want him to make me sad
Slowly I approached him one day
He invited me to talk to him and to stay

He talked of forgiveness
But his love caused my nearness

Questions for him I did begin
Many an hour we did share
In his heart I knew he did care

I did not think he knew what I did
Disguised I thought I had done real well
The core of me I thought I had hid
The filth inside I thought he would never smell

After we would talk and share
New lovers and pleasure I did snare
But never once did he say
Mary this must go away

Then each lover I did take
His face I saw it was no mistake
I want to give him this part of me
The pleasure I could grant to thee

He was different, to others more and more
His body I wanted for sure
My body he told me that he did not need
And that my soul he would always keep

"Mean Dog"

I would walk five miles to get ice cream from sonic
My sister worked there and it was for us a frequent topic
My brother would walk with me to go get it
We had all day and it was better than to have to sit

We started down the road my brother and me
And for us it was an adventure to see what we would see
Most of the walking we didn't see really too much
Cars passing by us really close I could almost touch

There was however one place that I really would become afraid
A man's house with a mean dog by his side that he would stay
I could tell the dog was trained to attack other people
Even though the man lived next door to a church and steeple

One day the man was missing from view
Then the dog came running at me and I knew not what to do
I was so afraid that the dog would attack me today
I want to run and yet my feet did not move but did stay

The dog came at me but at the last moment did stop
All the sudden he did wag his tail, biting he was not
The next day I did quietly return for the dog to see
With a package full of "weenies" he decided to come home with me

Components of Missing

I can see that "missing" is such a combination of things.

First, it's **thinking** about someone. About how much of the life they are becoming. And how much you start to become vulnerable. Then it becomes a **_Need_**. *That person's perspective on things. Their way of thinking and seeing things the need to open us and disclose the most secret of things...But the victories of life and its failures.*

*Then I think it is **anticipating** seeing that someone again. Looking forward to what's up ahead.... To sharing and laughing... And holding that person. I think also it involves **remembering** looking back and laughing or sometimes crying over what's behind.*

Weary eyes listening to music late at night or dancing until dawn. Serious debaters of the issues of life and the problems that surround the world. The curiosity to see the world and how different it is from us.

And one last thing to the components of missing. And it's probably not the most cheerful. Missing involves, on the human plane, a little bit of fear. **Fear** that well you may never see that someone again. **Fear** that you may never get the chance to share everything inside. **Fear** that you may never get the chance to really share some very special moments together.

Mountainside

Retreating back up the mountainside
Seeking refuge again and places to hide
Safety of solitude, hiding and what one is now to seek
Feelings of pain, vulnerable and a little weak

The mountainside is a place knowing all to well
Being about the only protection, becoming now a shell
Coming off the mountainside once to see
If loving could work with someone else and me

Finding then not a feeling of wanting to run away
Fighting all fears because and wanting to just stay
Deeper happiness than was ever been known
Deeper love being shared and was between two grown

Yours is a love that is truly one to cherish
Before all of life's dreams seem quickly to perish
Most people living in the valley below
It is all they think and all they know

Back to the mountainside, maybe now is the time
Leaving the valley, and all the people behind
If love exists, hoping for miracles and a celestial sign
Slowly walking up the path, beginning again to climb

My Dirty Secrets

Buried deep within the pit of my soul
Is a story that I have never told
Staying hidden within me and can make me cold
Happening when I was close to 7 years old

Doing things that are called very bad
Causing pain and making me for years sad
Older now, and they really just make me mad
Happening by a man that was called my dad

How can a man I called "father" do such things
When I am too young to even know what they mean
Confusion growing up, realizing that life is not what they seem
Hiding secrets within my mind and losing respect and self esteem

Early years should only be for building a good foundation
Not being abused by someone I don't even now mention
No one can really understand my current situation
Releasing this dirty little secret would be my elation

.

Jerry D. Hayes

Lives in Myrtle Beach, South Carolina- The Father of four wonderful children. Tara, Melissa, Jeremy and Jordan Hayes.

The author can be reached at JerryHayes65@yahoo.com